FIRST PoemS

PETER BEDRICK BOOKS
2112 Broadway
New York, NY 10023
First American edition published 1994
Selection © Julia Eccleshare 1993
Illustrations © Selina Young 1993
All rights reserved.
Published by agreement with
ORCHARD BOOKS, London
A CIP catalog record of this book is
available from the Library of Congress
ISBN 0 87226-373-8
LC# 93-40894
Printed in Singapore

FIRST
Poems

Compiled by Julia Eccleshare
Illustrated by Selina Young

PETER BEDRICK BOOKS

NEW YORK

CONTENTS

THE FOUR FRIENDS

Ernest was an elephant, a great big fellow,
  Leonard was a lion with a six-foot tail,
George was a goat, and his beard was yellow,
  And James was a very small snail.

Leonard had a stall, and a great big strong one,
  Ernest had a manger, and its walls were thick,
George found a pen, but I think it was the wrong one,
  And James sat down on a brick.

Ernest started trumpeting, and cracked his manger,
  Leonard started roaring, and shivered his stall,
James gave the huffle of a snail in danger
  And nobody heard him at all.

Ernest started trumpeting and raised such a rumpus,
   Leonard started roaring and trying to kick,
James went a journey with the goat's new compass
   And he reached the end of his brick.

Ernest was an elephant and very well-intentioned,
   Leonard was a lion with a brave new tail,
George was a goat, as I think I have mentioned,
   But James was only a snail.

A. A. Milne

FANTASTIC FRIENDS

The Incredible Hulk came to tea.
Robin was with him too,
Batman stayed at home that night
Because his bat had flu.

Superman called to say hello
And Spiderman spun us a joke.
Dynamite Sue was supposed to come
But she went up in smoke.

The Invisible Man might have called,
But as I wasn't sure,
I left an empty chair and bun
Beside the kitchen door.

They signed my autograph book.
But I dropped it in the fire.
Now whenever I tell my friends
They say I'm a terrible liar.

But incredible people *do* call round
('Specially when I'm alone)
And if they don't, and I get bored,
I call them on the phone.

Brian Patten

ON SOME OTHER PLANET

On some other planet
near some other star,
there's a music-loving alien
who has a green estate car

On some other planet
on some far distant world,
there's a bright sunny garden
where a cat lies curled.

On some other planet
a trillion miles away,
there are parks and beaches
where young aliens play

On some other planet
in another time zone,
there are intelligent beings
who feel very much alone.

On some other planet
one that we can't see,
there must be one person
who's a duplicate of me.

John Rice

THE OWL AND THE PUSSY CAT

The Owl and the Pussy Cat went to sea
  In a beautiful pea-green boat,
They took some honey, and plenty of money,
  Wrapped up in a five-pound note.
The Owl looked up to the stars above,
  And sang to a small guitar,
"O lovely Pussy! O Pussy, my love,
  What a beautiful Pussy you are,
    You are,
    You are!
What a beautiful Pussy you are!"

Pussy said to the Owl, "You elegant fowl!
  How charmingly sweet you sing!
O let us be married! Too long we have tarried:
  But what shall we do for a ring?"
They sailed away, for a year and a day,
  To the land where the Bong-tree grows
And there in a wood, a Piggy-wig stood
  With a ring at the end of his nose,
    His nose,
    His nose,
With a ring at the end of his nose.

"Dear Pig, are you willing to sell for one shilling
  Your ring?" Said the Piggy, "I will."
So they took it away, and were married next day
  By the Turkey who lives on the hill.
They dined on mince, and slices of quince,
  Which they ate with a runcible spoon;
And hand in hand, on the edge of the sand,
  They danced by the light of the moon,
    The moon,
    The moon,
They danced by the light of the moon.

Edward Lear

I Love My Darling Tractor

I love my darling tractor
I love its merry din,
Its muscles made of iron and steel,
Its red and yellow skin.

I love to watch its wheels go round
However hard the day,
And from its bed inside the shed
It never thinks to stray.

It saves my arm, it saves my leg,
It saves my back from toil,
And it's merry as a skink
      when I give it a drink
Of water and diesel oil.

I love my darling tractor
As you can clearly see,
And so, the jolly farmer said,
Would you if you were me.

Charles Causley

On The Skateboard

Skimming
an asphalt sea
I swerve, I curve, I
sway; I speed to whirring
sound an inch above the
ground; I'm the sailor
and the sail, I'm the
driver and the wheel
I'm the one and only
single engine
human auto
mobile.

Lillian Morrison

THE SKATEBOARD

My Daddy has bought me a skateboard;
He tried it out first at the store.
And that is the reason why
Mommy says Daddy can't walk any more.

Willard Espy

MOTORWAY WITCH

Here comes the witch.
She's not on her broom
But riding a motor bike
Going ZOOM . . . ZOOM . . . !

She's wearing a helmet
Instead of a hat
And there on the pillion
Is sitting her cat.

Please, no overtaking
For I should explain
With her speed-crazy cat
She prefers the fast lane.

She banished her broom
For that was her wish.
It wouldn't . . . ZOOM . . . ZOOM . . .
But only swish . . . swish!

Max Fatchen

ABC OF NAMES

A is Ann, with milk from the cow.

B is Benjamin, making a row.

C is Charlotte, gathering flowers.

D is Dick, one of the mowers.

E is Eliza, feeding a hen.

F is Frank, mending his pen.

G is Georgiana, shooting an arrow.

H is Harry, wheeling a barrow.

I is Isabella, gathering fruit.

J is John, playing the flute.

K is Kate, nursing her dolly.

L is Lawrence, feeding poor Polly.

M is Maria, learning to draw.

ABC of Names

N is Nicholas, with a jackdaw.

P is for Peter, wearing a coat.

R is Rachel, learning to dance.

T is Tommy, reading a book.

V is Victoria, reading she's seen.

X is Xerxes, a boy of great might.

Z is Zachariah, going to bed.

O is Octavus, riding a goat.

Q is for Quintus, armed with a lance.

S is Sarah, talking to Cook.

U is Urban, rolling the green.

W is Walter, flying a kite.

Y is Yvonne, a girl who's been fed.

Anon

MARY AND SARAH

Mary likes smooth things,
Things that glide:
Sleek skis swishing down a mountainside.

Sarah likes rough things,
Things that snatch:
Boats with barnacled bottoms, thatch.

Mary likes smooth things,
Things all mellow:
Milk, silk, runny honey, tunes on a cello.

Sarah likes rough things,
Things all troubly:
Crags, snags, bristles, thistles, fields left stubbly.

Mary says – polish,
Sarah says – rust,
Mary says – mayonnaise,
Sarah says – crust.

Sarah says – hedgehogs,
Mary says – seals,
Sarah says – sticklebacks,
Mary says – eels.

Give me, says Mary,
The slide of a stream,
The touch of a petal,
A bowl of ice-cream.

Give me, says Sarah,
The gales of a coast,
The husk of a chestnut,
A plate of burnt toast.

Mary and Sarah –
They'll never agree
Till peaches and coconuts
Grow on one tree.

Richard Edwards

THE KING'S BREAKFAST

The King asked
The Queen, and
The Queen asked
The Dairymaid:
"Could we have some butter for
The Royal slice of bread?"
The Queen asked
The Dairymaid,
The Dairymaid
Said,"Certainly,
I'll go and tell
The cow
Now
Before she goes to bed."

The Dairymaid
She curtsied,
And went and told
The Alderney:
"Don't forget the butter for
The Royal slice of bread."
The Alderney
Said sleepily:
"You'd better tell
His Majesty
That many people nowadays
Like marmalade
Instead."

The Dairymaid
Said, "Fancy!"
And went to
Her Majesty.
She curtsied to the Queen, and
She turned a little red:
"Excuse me,
Your Majesty,
For taking of
The liberty,
But marmalade is tasty, if
It's very
Thickly
Spread."

The Queen said,
"Oh !"
And went to
His Majesty:
"Talking of the butter for
The Royal slice of bread,
Many people
Think that
Marmalade
Is nicer.
Would you like to try a little
Marmalade
Instead?"

The King said,
"Bother !"
And then he said,
"Oh deary me!"
The King sobbed, "Oh, deary me!"
And went back to bed.
"Nobody,"
He whimpered,
"Could call me
A fussy man;
I *only* want
A little bit
Of butter for
My bread!"

The Queen said,
"There, there!"
And went to
The Dairymaid.
The Dairymaid
Said, "There, there!"
And went to the shed.
The cow said,
"There, there!
I didn't really
Mean it;
Here's milk for his porringer
And butter for his bread."

The Queen took
The butter
And brought it to
His Majesty;
The King said,
"Butter, eh?"
And bounced out of bed.
"Nobody," he said,
As he kissed her
Tenderly,
"Nobody," he said,
As he slid down
The banisters,
"Nobody,
My darling,
Could call me
A fussy man –
BUT
I do like a little bit of butter to my bread!"

A. A. Milne

FAIRY STORY

I went into the wood one day
And there I walked and lost my way

When it was so dark I could not see
A little creature came to me

He said if I would sing a song
The time would not be very long

But first I must let him hold my hand tight.
Or else the wood would give me a fright

I sang a song, he let me go
But now I am home again there is nobody I know.

Stevie Smith

LITTLE GIRL
(from an Arabian nursery rhyme)

I will build you a house
If you do not cry
A house, little girl,
As tall as the sky.

I will build you a house
Of golden dates,
The freshest of all
For the steps and gates.

I will furnish the house,
For you and for me
With walnuts and hazels
Fresh from the tree.

I will build you a house
And when it is done
I will roof it with grapes
To keep out the sun.

Rose Fyleman

SOME THINGS DON'T MAKE ANY SENSE AT ALL

My mom says I'm her sugarplum.
My mom says I'm her lamb.
My mom says I'm completely perfect
Just the way I am.
My mom says I'm a super-special wonderful terrific little guy.
My mom just had another baby.
Why?

Judith Viorst

THE BABY OF THE FAMILY

Up on Daddy's shoulders
He is riding high –
The baby of the family,
A pleased, pork pie.
I'm tired and my feet are sore –
It seems all wrong.
He's lucky to be little
But it won't last long.

The baby of the family,
He grabs my toys
And when I grab them back he makes
A big, loud noise.
I mustn't hit him, so I chant
This short, sweet song:
"You're lucky to be little
But it won't last long."

Everybody looks at him
And thinks he's sweet,
Even when he bellows "No!"
And stamps his feet.
He won't be so amusing
When he's tall and strong.
It's lovely being little
But it won't last long.

Wendy Cope

WHEN I WAS THREE

When I was three I had a friend
Who asked me why bananas bend,
I told him why, but now I'm four,
I'm not so sure . . .

Richard Edwards

MY SISTER LAURA

My sister Laura's bigger than me
And lifts me up quite easily.
I can't lift her, I've tried and tried;
She must have something heavy inside.

Spike Milligan

BETTY AT THE PARTY

"When I was at the party,"
  Said Betty, aged just four,
"A little girl fell off her chair
  Right down upon the floor;
And all the other little girls
  Began to laugh, but me –
I didn't laugh a single bit,"
  Said Betty seriously.

"Why not?" her mother asked her,
  Full of delight to find
That Betty – bless her little heart! –
  Had been so sweetly kind.
"Why didn't you laugh, my darling?
  Or don't you like to tell?"
"I didn't laugh," said Betty,
  "'Cause it was me that fell."

Anon

27

LAUGHING TIME

It was laughing time, and the tall Giraffe
Lifted his head, and began to laugh:

Ha! Ha! Ha! Ha!

And the Chimpanzee on the ginkgo tree
Swung merrily down with a Tee Hee Hee:

Hee! Hee! Hee! Hee!

"It's certainly not against the law!"
Croaked Justice Crow with a loud guffaw:

Haw! Haw! Haw! Haw!

The dancing Bear who could never say "No"
Waltzed up and down on the tip of his toe:

Ho! Ho! Ho! Ho!

The Donkey daintily took his paw,
And around they went: Hee-Haw! Hee-Haw!

Hee-Haw! Hee-Haw!

The Moon had to smile as it started to climb;
All over the world it was laughing time!

Ho! Ho! Ho! Ho! Hee-Haw! Hee-Haw!

Hee! Hee! Hee! Hee! Ha! Ha! Ha! Ha!

William Jay Smith

FIVE LITTLE OWLS

Five little owls in an old elm tree,
Fluffy and puffy as owls could be,
Blinking and winking with big round eyes
At the big round moon that hung in the skies:
As I passed beneath I could hear one say,
"There'll be mouse for supper, there will, today!"
Then all of them hooted, "Tu-whit, tu-whoo
Yes, mouse for supper, hoo hoo, hoo hoo!"

Anon

TEN LITTLE MICE

Ten little mice sat in a barn to spin,
Pussy came by, and popped her head in:
"What are you at, my jolly ten?"
"We're making coats for gentlemen."
"Shall I come in and cut your threads?"
"No, Miss Puss, you'd bite off our heads."

Anon

JIM, WHO RAN AWAY FROM HIS NURSE, AND WAS EATEN BY A LION

There was a boy whose name was Jim;
His friends were very good to him.
They gave him tea, and cakes, and jam,
And slices of delicious ham,
And chocolate with pink inside,
And little tricycles to ride,
And read him stories through and through,
And even took him to the Zoo
But there it was a dreadful fate
Befell him, which I now relate.

You know – at least you *ought* to know,
For I have often told you so –
That children never are allowed
To leave their nurses in a crowd;
Now this was Jim's especial foible,
He ran away when he was able,
And on this inauspicious day
He slipped his hand and ran away!
He hadn't gone a yard when – Bang!
With open jaws, a lion sprang,
And hungrily began to eat
The boy: beginning at his feet.

Now just imagine how it feels
When first your toes and then your heels,
And then by gradual degrees,
Your shins and ankles, calves and knees,
Are slowly eaten, bit by bit.
No wonder Jim detested it!
No wonder that he shouted "Hi!"
The honest keeper heard his cry,
Though very fat he almost ran
To help the little gentleman.
"Ponto!" he ordered as he came
(For Ponto was the lion's name),
"Ponto!" he cried, with angry frown.
"Let go, Sir! Down, Sir! Put it down!"

The lion made a sudden stop,
He let the dainty morsel drop,
And slunk reluctant to his cage,
Snarling with disappointed rage.
But when he bent him over Jim,
The honest keeper's eyes were dim.
The lion having reached his head,
The miserable boy was dead!

When Nurse informed his parents, they
Were more concerned than I can say:
His mother, as she dried her eyes,
Said, "Well – it gives me no surprise,
He would not do as he was told!"
His Father, who was self-controlled,
Bade all the children round attend
To James's miserable end,
And always keep a-hold of Nurse
For fear of finding something worse.

Hilaire Belloc

THE GREEDY ALLIGATOR

I have a rather greedy pet,
A little alligator;
When he my younger sister met,
He opened wide and ate her.

But soon he learned that he was wrong
To eat the child in question
For he felt bad before too long,
And suffered indigestion.

This story seems to prove to me
That he who rudely gobbles
Will soon regret his gluttony
And get the collywobbles.

Colin West

THE TIGER

A tiger going for a stroll
Met an old man and ate him whole.

The old man shouted, and he thumped.
The tiger's stomach churned and bumped.

The other tigers said: "Now really
We hear your breakfast much too clearly."

The moral is, he should have chewed.
It does no good to bolt one's food.

Edward Lucie-Smith

CALL ALLIGATOR LONG-MOUTH

Call alligator long-mouth
call alligator saw-mouth
call alligator pushy-mouth
call alligator scissors-mouth
call alligator raggedy-mouth
call alligator bumpy-bum
call alligator all dem rude word
but better wait

till you cross river.

John Agard

THE PLAINT OF THE CAMEL

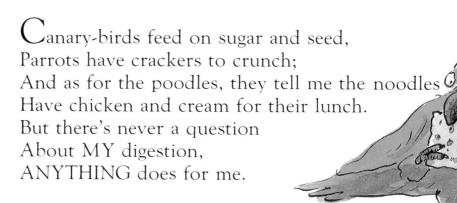

Canary-birds feed on sugar and seed,
Parrots have crackers to crunch;
And as for the poodles, they tell me the noodles
Have chicken and cream for their lunch.
But there's never a question
About MY digestion,
ANYTHING does for me.

Cats, you're aware, can repose in a chair,
Chickens can roost upon rails;
Puppies are able to sleep in a stable,
And oysters can slumber in pails.
But no one supposes
A poor Camel dozes.
ANY PLACE does for me.

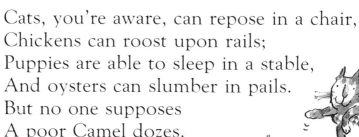

Lambs are enclosed where it's never exposed,
Coops are constructed for hens;
Kittens are treated to houses well heated,
And pigs are protected by pens.
But a Camel comes handy
Wherever it's sandy,
ANYWHERE does for me.

People would laugh if you rode a giraffe,
Or mounted the back of an ox;
It's nobody's habit to ride on a rabbit,
Or try to bestraddle a fox.
But as for a Camel, he's
Ridden by families –
ANY LOAD does for me.

A snake is as round as a hole in the ground;
Weasels are wavy and sleek;
And no alligator could ever be straighter
Than lizards that live in a creek.
But a Camel's all lumpy,
And bumpy, and humpy,
ANY SHAPE does for me.

Charles Edward Carryl

THE GUPPY

Whales have calves,
Cats have kittens,
Bears have cubs,
Bats have bittens.
Swans have cygnets,
Seals have puppies,
But guppies just have little guppies.

Ogden Nash

35

SNAIL

Snail upon the wall,
Have you got at all
Anything to tell
About your shell?

Only this, my child –
When the wind is wild,
Or when the sun is hot,
It's all I've got.

John Drinkwater

M was once a little mouse.
　　Mousey,
　　Bousy,
　　Sousy,
　　Mousy.
In the housy,
　　Little mouse!

Edward Lear

A BABY SARDINE

A baby sardine
Saw her first submarine:
She was scared and watched through a peephole.

"Oh come, come, come,"
Said the sardine's mum.
"It's only a tin full of people."

Spike Milligan

YAK

The long-haired Yak has long black hair,
He lets it grow – he doesn't care.
He lets it grow and grow and grow,
He lets it trail along the stair
Does he ever go to the barbershop? NO!
How wild and woolly and devil-may-care
A long-haired Yak with long black hair
Would look when perched in a barber chair!

William Jay Smith

BARBER

FROG

A frog once went out walking,
In the pleasant summer air,
He happened into a barber's shop
And skipped into the chair.
The barber said in disbelief;
"Your brains are surely bare.
How can you have a haircut
When you haven't any hair?"

Anon

A Frog he Would A-Wooing Go

A frog he would a-wooing go,
 Heigh ho! says Rowley,
A frog he would a-wooing go,
Whether his mother would let him or no.
 With a rowley, powley, gammon and spinach,
 Heigh ho! says Anthony Rowley.

So off he set with his opera hat,
 Heigh ho! says Rowley,
So off he set with his opera hat,
And on the road he met with a rat,
 With a rowley, powley, gammon and spinach,
 Heigh ho! says Anthony Rowley

Pray, Mr Rat, will you go with me?
 Heigh ho! says Rowley,
Pray, Mr Rat, will you go with me,
Kind Mrs Mousey for to see?
 With a rowley, powley, gammon and spinach,
 Heigh ho! says Anthony Rowley.

They came to the door of Mousey's hall,
 Heigh ho! says Rowley,
They gave a loud knock, and they gave a loud call.
 With a rowley, powley, gammon and spinach,
 Heigh ho! says Anthony Rowley.

Pray, Mrs Mouse, are you within?
 Heigh ho! says Rowley,
Oh yes, kind sirs, I'm sitting to spin.
 With a rowley, powley, gammon and spinach,
 Heigh ho! says Anthony Rowley.

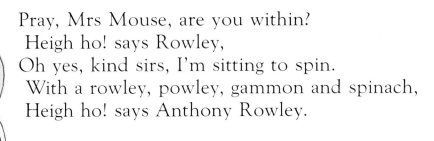

Pray, Mrs Mouse, will you give us some beer?
 Heigh ho! says Rowley,
For Froggy and I are fond of good cheer.
 With a rowley, powley, gammon and spinach,
 Heigh ho! says Anthony Rowley.

Pray, Mr Frog, will you give us a song?
 Heigh ho! says Rowley,
Let it be something that's not very long.
 With a rowley, powley, gammon and spinach,
 Heigh ho! says Anthony Rowley.

Indeed, Mrs Mouse, replied Mr Frog,
 Heigh ho! says Rowley,
A cold has made me as hoarse as a dog.
 With a rowley, powley, gammon and spinach,
 Heigh ho! says Anthony Rowley.

Since you have a cold, Mr Frog, Mousey said,
 Heigh ho! says Rowley,
I'll sing you a song that I have just made.
 With a rowley, powley, gammon and spinach,
 Heigh ho! says Anthony Rowley.

But while they were all a-merry-making,
 Heigh ho! says Rowley,
A cat and her kittens came tumbling in.
 With a rowley, powley, gammon and spinach,
 Heigh ho! says Anthony Rowley.

The cat she seized the rat by the crown,
 Heigh ho! says Rowley,
The kittens they pulled the little mouse down.
 With a rowley, powley, gammon and spinach,
 Heigh ho! says Anthony Rowley.

This put Mr Frog in a terrible fright,
 Heigh ho! says Rowley,
He took up his hat and he wished them good-night.
 With a rowley, powley, gammon and spinach,
 Heigh ho! says Anthony Rowley.

But as Froggy was crossing over a brook,
 Heigh ho! says Rowley,
A lily-white duck came and gobbled him up.
 With a rowley, powley, gammon and spinach,
 Heigh ho! says Anthony Rowley.

So there was an end of one, two, three,
 Heigh ho! says Rowley,
The rat, the mouse, and the little frog-ee.
 With a rowley, powley, gammon and spinach,
 Heigh ho! says Anthony Rowley.

Anon

BEAUTIFUL SOUP

Beautiful Soup, so rich and green,
  Waiting in a hot tureen!
Who for such dainties would not stoop?
Soup of the evening, beautiful Soup!
Soup of the evening, beautiful Soup!
  Beau – ootiful Soo – oop!
  Beau – ootiful Soo – oop!
Soo – oop of the e – e – evening,
  Beautiful, beautiful Soup!

Beautiful Soup! Who cares for fish,
  Game, or any other dish?
Who would not give all else for two p
ennyworth only of beautiful Soup?
Pennyworth only of beautiful Soup?
  Beau – ootiful Soo – oop!
  Beau – ootiful Soo – oop!
Soo – op of the e – e – evening,
Beautiful, beauti-FUL SOUP!

Lewis Carroll

PEAS

I always eat peas with honey,
I've done it all my life,
They do taste kind of funny
But it keeps them on the knife.

Anon

IF ALL THE WORLD
WERE PAPER

If all the world were paper,
  And all the sea were ink,
And all the trees were bread and cheese,
  What should we do for drink?

Anon

THE FOLK WHO LIVE IN
BACKWARD TOWN

The folk who live in Backward Town
Are inside out and upside down.
They wear their hats inside their heads
And go to sleep beneath their beds.
They only eat the apple peeling
And take their walks across the ceiling.

Mary Ann Hoberman

AS WET AS A FISH

As wet as a fish – as dry as a bone;
As live as a bird – as dead as a stone;
As plump as a partridge – as poor as a rat;
As strong as a horse – as weak as a cat;
As hard as a flint – as soft as a mole;
As white as a lily – as black as a coal;
As plain as a pike-staff – as rough as a bear;
As tight as a drum – as free as the air;
As heavy as lead – as light as a feather;
As steady as time – uncertain as weather;
As hot as a furnace – as cold as a frog;
As gay as a lark – as sick as a dog;
As slow as a tortoise – as swift as the wind;
As true as the gospel – as false as mankind;
As thin as a herring – as fat as a pig;
As proud as a peacock – as blithe as a grig;
As fierce as a tiger – as mild as a dove;
As stiff as a poker – as limp as a glove;
As blind as a bat – as deaf as a post;
As cool as a cucumber – as warm as a toast;
As flat as a flounder – as round as a ball;
As blunt as a hammer – as sharp as an awl;
As red as a ferret – as safe as the stocks;
As bold as a thief – as sly as a fox;
As straight as an arrow – as bent as a bow;
As yellow as saffron – as black as a sloe;
As brittle as glass – as tough as gristle;
As neat as my nail – as clean as a whistle;
As good as a feast – as bad as a witch;
As light as is day – as dark as is pitch;
As brisk as a bee – as dull as an ass;
As full as a tick – as solid as brass.

Anon

ME AND THE EARTHWORM

Me: Where are you going, Earthworm?
Earthworm: Around the world.

Me: How long will it take?
Earthworm: A long stretch.

Zaro Weil

SQUEEZES

We love to squeeze bananas,
We love to squeeze ripe plums.
And when they are feeling sad
We love to squeeze our mums.

Brian Patten

I'D LIKE TO SQUEEZE

I'd like to squeeze this round world
into a new shape

I'd like to squeeze this round world
like a tube of toothpaste

I'd like to squeeze this round world
fair and square

I'd like to squeeze it and squeeze it
till everybody had an equal share

John Agard

MY SHADOW

I have a little shadow that goes in and out with me,
And what can be the use of him is more than I can see.
He is very, very like me from the heels up to the head;
And I see him jump before me, when I jump into my bed.

The funniest thing about him is the way he likes to grow –
Not at all like proper children, which is always very slow;
For he sometimes shoots up taller like an india-rubber ball,
And he sometimes gets so little that there's none of him at all.

He hasn't got a notion of how children ought to play,
And can only make a fool of me in every sort of way.
He stays so close beside me, he's a coward you can see;
I'd think shame to stick to nursie as that shadow sticks to me!

One morning, very early, before the sun was up,
I rose and found the shining dew on every buttercup;
But my lazy little shadow, like an arrant sleepy-head,
Had stayed at home behind me and was fast asleep in bed.

Robert Louis Stevenson

EVERY TIME I CLIMB A TREE

Every time I climb a tree
Every time I climb a tree
Every time I climb a tree
I scrape a leg
Or skin a knee
And every time I climb a tree
I find some ants
Or dodge a bee
And get the ants
All over me.

And every time I climb a tree
Where have you been?
They say to me
But don't they know that I am free
Every time I climb a tree?
I like it best
To spot a nest
That has an egg
Or maybe three.

And then I skin
The other leg
But every time I climb a tree
I see a lot of things to see
Swallows rooftops and TV
And all the fields and farms there be
Every time I climb a tree.
Though climbing may be good for ants
It isn't awfully good for pants
But still it's pretty good for me
Every time I climb a tree.

David McCord

THE UPS AND DOWNS OF THE ELEVATOR CAR

The elevator car in the elevator shaft,
Complained of the buzzer, complained of the draught.
It said it felt carsick as it rose and fell,
It said it had a headache from the ringing of the bell.

"There is spring in the air," sighed the elevator car.
Said the elevator man, "You are well off where you are."
The car paid no attention but it frowned an ugly frown

                     when
             up   it
       going   should
    started   be
  it   going
And   down.

Down flashed the signal, but *up* went the car.
The elevator man cried, "You are going much too far!"
Said the elevator car, "I'm doing no such thing.
I'm through with buzzers buzzing. I'm looking for the spring !"

Then the elevator man began to shout and call
And all the people came running through the hall.
The elevator man began to call and shout.
"The car won't stop! Let me out! Let me out!"

On went the car past the penthouse door.
On went the car up one flight more.
On went the elevator till it came to the top.
On went the elevator, and it would not stop!

Right through the roof went the man and the car.
And nobody knows where the two of them are!
(Nobody knows but everyone cares,
Wearily, drearily climbing the stairs!)

Now on a summer evening when you see a shooting star
Fly through the air, perhaps it is – that elevator car!

Caroline D. Emerson

THE JUMBLIES

They went to sea in a Sieve, they did,
 In a Sieve they went to sea:
In spite of all their friends could say,
On a winter's morn, on a stormy day,
 In a Sieve they went to sea!
And when the Sieve turned round and round,
And every one cried, "You'll all be drowned!"
They called aloud, "Our Sieve ain't big,
But we don't care a button! we don't care a fig!
 In a Sieve we'll go to sea!"
 Far and few, far and few,
  Are the lands where the Jumblies live;
  Their heads are green, and their hands are blue
  And they went to sea in a Sieve.

They sailed away in a Sieve, they did,
 In a Sieve they sailed so fast,
With only a beautiful pea-green veil
Tied with a riband by way of a sail,
 To a small tobacco-pipe mast;
And every one said, who saw them go,
"Oh won't they be soon upset, you know!
For the sky is dark, and the voyage is long,
And happen what may, it's extremely wrong
 In a Sieve to sail so fast!"
  Far and few, far and few,
   Are the lands where the Jumblies live;
   Their heads are green, and their hands are blue,
    And they went to sea in a Sieve.

The water it soon came in, it did,
 The water it soon came in;
So to keep them dry, they wrapped their feet
In a pinky paper all folded neat,
 And they fastened it down with a pin
And they passed the night in a crockery-jar,
And each of them said, "How wise we are!
Though the sky be dark, and the voyage be long,
Yet we never can think we were rash or wrong,
 While round in our Sieve we spin!"
  Far and few, far and few,
   Are the lands where the Jumblies live;
   Their heads are green, and their hands are blue,
    And they went to sea in a Sieve.

And all night long they sailed away;
 And when the sun went down,
They whistled and warbled a moony song
To the echoing sound of a coppery gong,
 In the shade of the mountains brown.
"O Timballo! How happy we are,
When we live in a sieve and a crockery-jar,
And all night long in the moonlight pale,
We sail away with a pea-green sail,
 In the shade of the mountains brown!"
 Far and few, far and few,
  Are the lands where the Jumblies live;
 Their heads are green, and their hands are blue,
  And they went to sea in a Sieve.

waterproof pinky paper   pins   Crockery Jar.   Sieve

They sailed to the Western Sea, they did,
 To a land all covered with trees,
And they bought an Owl, and a useful Cart,
And a pound of Rice, and a Cranberry Tart,
 And a hive of silvery Bees.
And they bought a Pig, and some green Jack-daws
And a lovely Monkey with lollipop paws,
And forty bottles of Ring-Bo-Ree,
 And no end of Stilton Cheese.
 Far and few, far and few,
  Are the lands where the Jumblies live;
 Their heads are green, and their hands are blue,
  And they went to sea in a Sieve.

And in twenty years they all came back;
 In twenty years or more,
And every one said, "How tall they've grown!
For they've been to the Lakes, and the Torrible Zone,
 And the hills of the Chankly Bore";
And they drank their health, and gave them a feast
Of dumplings made of beautiful yeast;
And every one said, "If we only live,
We too will go to sea in a Sieve, –
 To the hills of the Chankly Bore!"
 Far and few, far and few,
  Are the lands where the Jumblies live;
 Their heads are green, and their hands are blue,
  And they went to sea in a Sieve.

Edward Lear

Until I Saw the Sea

Until I saw the sea
I did not know
that wind
could wrinkle water so.

I never knew
that sun
could splinter a whole sea of blue.

Nor
did I know before,
a sea breathes in and out
upon a shore.

Lilian Moore

Listen

Shhhhhhhhhhhhhhhhhhhhhhhhhhhhhh!
Sit still, very still
And listen.
Listen to wings
Lighter than eyelashes
Stroking the air.
Know what the thin breeze
Whispers on high
To the coconut trees.
Listen and hear.

Telcine Turner

BALLOON

```
        a s
      big as
    ball as round
  as sun . . . I tug
and pull you when
you run and when
  wind blows I
    say polite
        ly
         H
          O
          L
          D
          M
          E
          T
          I
           G
            H
             T
              L
               Y.
```

Colleen Thibaudeau

SUMMER

When it's hot
I take my shoes off,
I take my shirt off,
I take my pants off,
I take my underwear off,
I take my whole body off,
and throw it
in the river.

Frank Asch

MUD

I like mud.
  I like it on my clothes.
I like it on my fingers.
  I like it in my toes.

Dirt's pretty ordinary
  And dust's a dud.
For a really good mess-up
  I like mud.

John Smith

BUSY DAY

Pop in
pop out
pop over the road
pop out for a walk
pop in for a talk
pop down to the shop
can't stop
got to pop

got to pop ?

pop where?
pop what?

well
I've got to
pop round
pop up
pop in to town
pop out and see
pop in for tea
pop down to the shop
can't stop
got to pop

got to pop?

pop where?
pop what?

well
I've got to
pop in
pop out
pop over the road
pop out for a walk
pop in for a talk . . .

Michael Rosen

THE SNOWMAN

Mother, while you were at the shops
and I was snoozing in my chair
I heard a tap at the window
saw a snowman standing there

He looked so cold and miserable
I almost could have cried
so I put the kettle on
and invited him inside

I made him a cup of cocoa
to warm the cockles of his nose
then he snuggled in front of the fire
for a cosy little doze

He lay there warm and smiling
softly counting sheep
I eavesdropped for a little while
then I too fell asleep

Seems he awoke and tiptoed out
exactly when I'm not too sure
it's a wonder you didn't see him
as you came in through the door

(Oh, and by the way,
the kitten's made a puddle on the floor)

Roger McGough

SOMEONE

Someone came knocking
At my wee, small door;
Someone came knocking,
I'm sure – sure – sure;
I listened, I opened,
I looked to left and right,
But nought there was a-stirring
In the still dark night;
Only the busy beetle
Tap-tapping in the wall,
Only from the forest
The screech-owl's call,
Only the cricket whistling
While the dewdrops fall,
So I know not who came knocking,
At all, at all, at all.

Walter de la Mare

WHO'S IN ?

"The door is shut fast
  And everybody's out.
But people don't know
  What they're talking about!
Say the fly on the wall,
And the flame on the coals,
And the dog on his rug.
And the mice in their holes,
And the kitten curled up,
And the spiders that spin –
"What, everyone out?
Why, everyone's in!"

Elizabeth Fleming

THE LAND OF NOD

From breakfast on through all the day
At home among my friends I stay;
But every night I go abroad
Afar into the Land of Nod.

All by myself I have to go,
With none to tell me what to do –
All alone beside the streams
And up the mountain-sides of dreams.

The strangest things are there for me,
Both things to eat and things to see,
And many frightening sights abroad
Till morning in the Land of Nod.

Try as I like to find the way,
I never can get back by day,
Nor can remember plain and clear
The curious music that I hear.

Robert Louis Stevenson

NIGHT COMES

Night comes
leaking
out of the sky.

Stars come
peeking.

Moon comes
sneaking
silvery-sly.

Who is
shaking,
shivery,
quaking?

Who is afraid
of the night?

Not I.

Beatrice Schenk de Regniers

SWEET DREAMS

I wonder as into bed I creep
What it feels like to fall asleep.
I've told myself stories, I've counted sheep
But I'm always asleep when I fall asleep.
Tonight my eyes I will open keep,
And I'll stay awake till I fall asleep,
Then I'll know what it feels like to fall asleep,
Asleep,
Asleeep,
Asleeeep . . .

Ogden Nash

MOONING

What shall we do? O what can we do?
The Man in the Moon has lost his shoe –

We'll search all night on the rubbish-dump
For a star-spangled sneaker or a moon-bright pump.

What shall we do? O what can we do?
Now he's gone and lost his trousers too.

We'll search all night and hope to find
Something that will warm his bare behind.

It's a bit strange and it's a bit sad
But the Man in the Moon has gone quite mad.

He is flinging away all his clothes
And where they'll end up nobody knows.

So don't look at the sky. don't look, it's rude –
The Man in the Moon is completely nude!

Brian Patten

MRS MOON

Mrs Moon
sitting up in the sky
Little Old Lady
rock-a-bye
with a ball of fading light
and silvery needles
knitting the night.

Roger McGough

THE HORSEMAN

I heard a horseman
Ride over the hill;
The moon shone clear,
The night was still;
His helm was silver,
And pale was he,
And the horse he rode
Was of ivory.

Walter de la Mare

INDEX OF AUTHORS AND TITLES

ACKNOWLEDGEMENTS

The compiler and publishers wish to thank all the poets, agents, publishers and other copyright holders who kindly granted us permission to use the poems in this anthology.

"The Four Friends", "The King's Breakfast" from *When We Were Very Young* by A.A. Milne. © 1924 by E.P. Dutton, renewed 1952 by A.A. Milne. Used by permission of Dutton Children's Books, a division of Penguin Books USA Inc. "Billy Dreamer's Fantastic Friends" © Brian Patten, reprinted by permission of the author. "On Some Other Planet" © John Rice, reprinted by permission of the author. "I Love my Darling Tractor" from *Early in the Morning* by Charles Causley, reprinted by permission of David Higham Associates. "On the Skateboard" from *The Sidewalk Racer and Other Poems of Sport and Motion* by Lillian Morrison, © 1965, 1968, 1977 Lillian Morrison, reprinted by permission of Marion Reiner for the author. "Motorway Witch" by Max Fatchen, reprinted by permission of John Johnson Ltd. "Mary and Sarah" from *A Mouse in My Roof* by Richard Edwards, published by Orchard Books, reprinted by permission of the author. "Fairy Story" by Stevie Smith from *The Collected Poems of Stevie Smith*. © 1972 by Stevie Smith. Reprinted by permission of New Directions Publishing Corp. "Little Girl" by Rose Fyleman, reprinted by permission of The Society of Authors as the literary representative of the Estate of Rose Fyleman. "Some Things Don't Make Any Sense At All" from *If I Were In Charge Of The World And Other Worries* published by Atheneum, an imprint of the Macmillan Publishing company, © 1981 Judith Viorst. "The Baby of the Family" by Wendy Cope from *Casting a Spell* published by Orchard Books, reprinted by permission of the author. "When I Was Three" by Richard Edwards from *The Word Party* published by Lutterworth Press, and reprinted by permission of the author. "My Sister Laura" and "The Baby Sardine" reprinted by permission of the author and Norma Farnes. "Laughing Time" and "Yak" from *Laughing Time: Collected Nonsense* by William Jay Smith, © 1990 William Jay Smith, reprinted by permission of Farrar, Straus and Giroux, Inc. "Jim Who Ran Away From His Nurse And Was Eaten by a Lion" by Hilaire Belloc, reprinted by permission of Peters, Fraser and Dunlop Group Ltd. "The Greedy Alligator" by Colin West, reprinted by permission of the author. "The Tiger" by Edward Lucie-Smith from *Beasts With Bad Manners*, reprinted by permission of Rogers, Coleridge and White Ltd. "Don't Call Alligator Long Mouth Till You Cross River" from *Say it Again Granny* published by The Bodley Head, © 1986 John Agard, reprinted by permission of John Agard c/o Caroline Sheldon Literary Agency. "The Guppy" from *Verses From 1929 On* by Ogden Nash. First appeared in The Saturday Evening Post. By permission from Little, Brown and Company. "Snail" by John Drinkwater, reprinted by permission of Samuel French Ltd on behalf of the Estate of the late John Drinkwater. "The Folk Who Live in Backward Town" by Mary Ann Hoberman from *Hello and Good-bye* published by Little Brown and Company, reprinted by permission of Gina Maccoby Literary Agency, © 1959, copyright renewed 1987 by Mary Ann Hoberman. "Me and the Earthworm" from *Mud, Moon and Me* published by Orchard Books, © 1989 Zaro Weil, reprinted by permission of the author. "Squeezes" from *Gargling with Jelly* published by Viking Kestrel, © 1985 Brian Patten, reprinted by permission of Rogers, Coleridge and White Ltd. "I'd Like to Squeeze" from *You'll Love This Stuff* published by Cambridge University Press 1986, reprinted by permission of John Agard c/o Caroline Sheldon Literary Agency. "Every Time I Climb a Tree" from *One At a Time* by David McCord. © 1952 by David McCord. By permission of Little, Brown and Company. "Until I Saw the Sea" from *I Feel The Same Way* by Lilian Moore, © 1967 Lilian Moore, reprinted by permission of Greenwillow Books, a division of William Morrow and Company, Inc. "Summer" from *Country Pie* by Frank Asch, © 1979 Frank Asch, reprinted by permisson of Greenwillow Books, a division of Wiliam Morrow and Company, Inc. "Busy Day" from You Tell Me by Michael Rosen and Roger McGough publihsed by Kestrel Books, © 1979 Michael Rosen, reprinted by permission of Penguin Books Ltd. "The Snowman" and "Mrs Moon" from *Sky in the Pie* by Roger McGough, reprinted by permission of the Peters Fraser and Dunlop Group Ltd. "Someone" and "The Horseman" by Walter de la Mare, reprinted by permission of the Literary Trustees of Walter de la Mare and The Society of Authors as their representative. "Night Comes" from *A Bunch of Poems and Verses* by Beatrice Schenk de Regniers, © 1977 Beatrice Schenk de Regniers, reprinted by permission of Marian Reiner for the author. "Sweet Dreams" by Ogden Nash from *The New Nutcracker Suite and Other Innocent Verses* published by Little, Brown and Company, © 1962 Ogden Nash, reprinted by permission of Curtis Brown Ltd. "Mooning" by Brian Patten from *Thawing Frozen Frogs* published by Viking Kestrel, © 1990 Brian Patten, reprinted by permission of Rogers, Coleridge and White Ltd.

Every effort has been made to trace all the copyright holders and the publishers apologise if any inadvertent omission has been made.